To: Us

An ADVENTurous Christmas Devotional

24 days to Christmas.

24 Christmas Characters.

Journey through the Old and New Testaments discovering God's plan for you in the Christmas story.

Teri Herndon

Travel Guide

Travel Guide 2

Itineration 5

Just a Shepherd 7

A Promise 10

Crazy Families and Firsts 13

Rescue Mission 16

Travel Plans 19

Gift Exchange 22

It's Complicated 24

Heaven and Earth 26

Silence 29

Slay It 32

Trust 35

Perspective 37

I Wonder 40

Unlikely People 43

Opportunities **45**

There's Hope **48**

Searching **51**

Not everyone **54**

The Good King **57**

The Promise **59**

Waiting Expectantly **62**

Amazing Love **64**

To: Us **66**

Prayer of Dedication **69**

Scripture quotes are from the New Living Translation
unless otherwise noted.

To my grandkids:

Norah, Isak, Dexter, Noah, Penny, Clive, and Emmitt.

Love you so much!

Jesus loves you even more!

December 1

Itineration

Welcome, to the ADVENTurous Christmas journey!

Over the years, I have been blessed to do a fair amount of traveling. My dad worked for United Airlines, and flying was in my blood. Before any trip, information is needed, and preparations are required. That was my mom's responsibility!

The length of the trip determines the size of the suitcase; the mode of transportation is also a factor. Trains, planes, and automobiles are not equal in luggage capacity. My husband, Jay, and I learned that the hard way when our suitcases didn't fit on the European trains!

When a church invites Jay to speak, his administrative assistant prepares an itineration folder. It tells us where we are heading and how long it will take to get there. It's very helpful, and I want to do the same for you! Consider this your itineration for this Christmas Devotional.

Our journey will take us to both the Old and New Testaments. Over the next 24 days, we will explore 24 Christmas characters. Some of the individuals are named in the genealogy of Jesus, including Tamar, Rahab, Ruth, and Bathsheba. You may be thinking, "Genealogy? Really?" I get it. Reading a list of people's names with no personal connection is not very exciting. However, I hope to make the genealogy of Jesus both personal and engaging as we read it through the eyes of Christmas.

We will visit all the traditional characters we associate with Christmas like Mary, Joseph, the angels, shepherds, and more. During the journey, our hosts will also include Boaz, Caesar Augustus, and King Herod.

There are other VIP Christmas characters to consider, and they are YOU and me! We are the reason Christmas came! "For unto US, a child is born. Unto US, a son is given!" (Is 9:6)

During this journey, there are a few things to keep in mind:

First, when traveling to a different country, it's a good idea to be familiar with a few essential words. You will come across the word Advent. If you're not familiar with what that is, it literally means "coming." Advent is the arrival of a notable person, thing, or event. (Oxford Languages)

This ADVENTurous Christmas Devotional is designed to prepare our hearts for the celebration of Jesus' arrival in Bethlehem. During this journey, there are lessons to be learned and challenges to consider. It will also remind us that there is yet another arrival to come—the 2nd Advent. Jesus said, "When everything is ready, I will come and get you, so that you will always be with Me where I am." (Jn 14:3)

Lastly, traveling over Christmas seems to be inevitable for many. And packing, that can be tricky. You often come home with more than you went with. In essence, that is what I hope for you. I pray that the suitcase of your soul will be fuller on December 24 than it is right now.

So, get ready. Tomorrow we begin!

December 2

Just a Shepherd

This is a record of the ancestors of Jesus the Messiah,
a descendant of ***DAVID*** *and of Abraham.*
Matthew 1:1

My husband Jay and I were planning an overseas trip, and our preparation included Jay researching his family tree. The Herndons had adopted Jay's dad as a young boy. Finding both adoptive and bloodline ancestor roots were therefore a bit tricky but very rewarding. With Scotland on our itinerary, it was exciting to learn that my guy comes from the bloodline of Robert the Bruce, King of Scotland. I always knew he was a prince!

David is the first person listed in the genealogy of Jesus, so that seems like a great place for us to start as well. 1 Samuel 16 tells us of a young shepherd who would become a king.

The Lord instructed Samuel to visit Jesse in *Bethlehem.* One of Jesse's sons would be chosen as the new king. Jesse presented his seven sons to the prophet, but the future king was not in this group. When Samuel asked if there were any other sons, Jesse told Samuel about his youngest, David, who was a *shepherd.* Samuel then demanded that Jesse bring David in from the field. The entire household *waited* for David's arrival - the one who would be anointed as king. As scripture introduces David to us, I see three words that ring Christmas: Bethlehem, Shepherd, and Waiting.

We read the word *Bethlehem*, and images of the Christmas story flood our imagination. But before that famous day, Bethlehem was just a tiny town. No one gave it much care or thought. But Jesus changed that!

If you are feeling like Bethlehem, unseen and uncared for, be encouraged. God sees you! God deeply cares for you! And just as Jesus came to Bethlehem, He desires to come to you.

Back to David! *Shepherds* play a vital part in the Christmas story. Christmas plays aren't complete without the cotton ball dressed little children and the feisty little shepherd boy with his oversized staff. Cute? Absolutely! But in ancient days, being a shepherd was a culturally unimportant but necessary job. Jesse did not even consider David as a possible candidate to be a king. It was as if Samuel's question reminded Jesse that he had another son. "David? Really? He's just a shepherd." Well, David wasn't "just" a shepherd. He was learning life lessons that would make him a compelling poet, a mighty warrior, and one of the most notable kings in history.

Friends, we are not "just" anything. We are not just stay-at-home moms, office employees, teachers, students, public workers, pastors, wives, or kids. We are in a place where we can learn and grow. God is equipping us now for whatever is next.

Lastly is *waiting*. Waiting for Christmas as a child was painful, and I wondered if it was ever going to arrive. As an adult, I've learned that waiting is a part of life. David waited in the shepherd's field. He waited in caves. He waited for God's timing to become king.

We wait, too. We wait for answers, direction, jobs, family, finances, healing, or help. Waiting isn't pleasant but necessary. When we wait in anticipation, we grow and mature. We develop patience and fortitude, strength, and peace. When we wait correctly, it creates a sense of excitement about the arrival. When we fight against waiting, we become frustrated, discouraged, and exhausted. And that's bah-humbug!

Not only do I see Christmas in David's story, but I see myself. That's the beauty of the Bible. It's personal!

Where do you see yourself? Wherever it is, remember, God can do tremendous things with just a shepherd!

December 3

A Promise

This is a record of the ancestors of Jesus the Messiah,
a descendant of David and of ***ABRAHAM****.*
Matthew 1:1

If you grew up in the church, chances are you sang "Father Abraham" a time or two. If you're not familiar with that "got it stuck in my head" tune, I am pretty sure it was responsible for launching the Christian aerobics movement!

This peppy children's song was inspired by a promise God made to Abraham. "I will bless you and make you famous, and you will be a blessing to others ... All the families on earth will be blessed through you." (Gen 12:2-3)

God did not give any indication of when this promise was to be fulfilled, but He did give Abraham some instructions. The Lord told Abraham to leave his country, his relatives, and his father's family and to go to a land where he had never been before. I imagine this was a difficult ask for Abraham. Culturally, families stayed together. Abraham was born, grew up, and married in the land of Ur. Life there was all he knew, and the Lord was asking Abraham to walk away. Literally.

Abraham was 75 when he and Sarah packed up all their belongings and headed to Canaan. God's ask may have been huge, but His promise was enormous. Abraham and Sarah clung to that promise of a son. It's what gave them the determination to continue, but after years of obedient journeying and waiting and no baby, Abraham and his wife got impatient. They had a brilliant idea. "Let's help God." That was a very bad idea, and Ishmael was born. He would be the brother from another mother. Ishmael was not God's promised plan so Abraham and Sarah had to continue to wait for the true promise.

Total wait time ... 25 years! That's a long time. We are impatient at stoplights. We want our promises now! But God has reasons for delays. Here, it highlights the miracle: Sarah was far past childbearing age. Isaac's birth was a true miracle! (Gen 21:1-7)

God's promise to Abraham, "In you all the families of the earth will be blessed,"(Gen 12:3 NKJV) is a direct reference to the birth of Jesus. That would happen 28 generations later. I don't think Abraham had any idea of the magnitude of God's promise!

Abraham's story is about *a promised blessing* and a miracle birth. Christmas is *the promised blessing* and a miracle birth.

Incredibly, God was thinking about the first Advent, Christmas, a couple of thousand years before it happened. That is seriously looking at the big picture! And with the same amount of detail, the second Advent is already planned. Jesus IS coming again. This time it will be to claim His bride, all those who love Him.

You may be approaching this Christmas with unfulfilled promises. Maybe you are even growing weary of the wait. Let's be encouraged by these two lessons in Abraham's story.

First, don't try to help God along with His plan. It won't work! But if this lesson is coming too late, no worries. God promises to work good in all things for those who love Him.

Secondly, if God said it, He WILL do it! Our job is to be obedient to what the Lord asks of us and then watch for the when and how. Like presents under the tree, God's promises rarely look like what we are expecting. They are far better than we can ever hope, dream, or imagine!

December 4

Crazy Families and Firsts

Judah was the father of Perez and Zerah
*(whose mother was **TAMAR**).*
Matthew 1:3

I am the first of four siblings and the first grandchild on both my sides of my family. I was also the first female minister from our District to be elected to the General Presbytery (the national governing board for the Assemblies of God). These are kinda big deals.

Tamar was the first woman to be listed in the genealogy of Jesus. That really *IS* a big deal! In ancient times, it was uncommon to have a woman listed in legal records. Tamar is the first, but she isn't the last.

Tamar is also the first woman to show us the customs and laws regarding widows who had no children. It was called the Levirate marriage. The brother of the deceased man was obligated to marry his sister-in-law. He would give her a son, and the son would have the rights of the dead father, thereby carrying on the family name. The brother also had the option of releasing the widow. That would give her the right to marry someone else, but in Tamar's case, neither law was fulfilled.

Warning: This is a bit of a soap opera.

After Tamar's husband Er died – well, God actually killed him - Er's younger brother Onan "slept" with her, but Onan made sure she wouldn't get pregnant. (I'm actually too embarrassed to write what the Bible literally says.) Because of that, Onan died. The youngest brother, Shelah, was then promised to Tamar, but Judah didn't fulfill that promise either. At this point, Tamar had few options. She needed a son to survive, and by law, it was her right. So she came up with a plan.

The wife of Judah, Tamar's father-in-law, died, and he became lonely. So Tamar decided to capitalize on that by pretending to be a prostitute. Judah did not recognize her, and unlike his son Onan, Judah did not take the same precautions. She became pregnant, and God blessed her with twin boys, Perez and Zerah. (Gen 38)

Okay, this is a crazy story! Especially when we read it through our 21st century western lens. Nevertheless, God chose Tamar's son, Perez, whose father is also his grandfather, to continue the Messianic lineage of Jesus. You can't make this stuff up!

We ALL have crazy family stories! But, the good news is, no person's story is too crazy for God to inhabit, restore, or use. As a matter of fact, it's His specialty!

Tamar's story of being a first reminds me of Christmas firsts. Some firsts are exciting, like the first Christmas in a new home or as a married couple or the first Christmas with a new fur baby, child, or grandchild. These are all big deals. Jesus rejoices with you!

However, even with all the holiday joy, there are some Christmas firsts that are not so pleasant. In fact, they are painful. Like when a loved one's chair at the table is empty or a holiday tradition isn't going to happen. These are also big deals. The loss is real. Jesus mourns with you and desires to comfort you.

If this Advent season finds you in the middle of a crazy family or experiencing a undesired first, I encourage you to pause and invite Jesus into the midst of it. He is more than able to handle it.

How will you respond?

December 5

Rescue Mission

Salmon was the father of Boaz
*(whose mother was **RAHAB**).*
Matthew 1:5

Rahab, the second woman listed in the genealogy of Jesus, is the story of a woman in need of rescue.

I'm a proud aunt of three nephews who are Air Force SERE Specialists. The oldest, Anthony, as a Special Operator, has been involved in overseas rescue missions. Much preparation, planning, and coordination are critical to each rescue. The same was the case with today's Christmas character, Rahab.

It's a long story, but the bottom line is that Rahab was trapped in prostitution and unable to escape without help. She needed someone to rescue her.

Joshua had sent two men to spy out the land and the city of Jericho. They just "happened" to go to Rahab's home to gain intel.

The unskilled spies were quickly identified as foreigners, and the king was told of their presence. However, Rahab hid the men and lied to the king's men as to their whereabouts. That was risky, but her faith was stronger.

Rahab declared to Joshua's men: "... for the Lord your God is the supreme God of the heavens above and the earth below. Now swear to me by the Lord that you will be kind to me and my family since I have helped you. Give me some guarantee that when Jericho is conquered, you will let me live, along with my father and mother, my brothers and sisters, and all their families." (Josh 2:11-13)

The spies agreed to Rahab's request. They set the conditions and laid out the plan, including a scarlet cord hanging from her city wall window. Rahab and her family had to be in the right place at the right time if they had any hope of surviving. (Josh 2:17-18)

Jericho's walls were designed to protect the city and provide housing in its massive structure. At God's appointed time, the walls of Jericho began to collapse. It must have felt like an earthquake! The enormous walls were falling, and against all-natural instinct, Rahab stayed put inside the wall. The Israelites rushed in, destroying the entire city and capturing its residents – all while Rahab awaited her rescuers. Joshua's men had successfully executed the mission! (Josh 6)

Rahab and her family were the only survivors, and they agreed to live among the Jewish people. In time, Rahab then married Salmon and became the great, great-grandmother of King David! (Matt 1:5)

Like Rahab, we, too, need rescuing. Christmas was the beginning of that rescue mission! The plan took 33 years to complete, and Jesus executed it perfectly!

The scarlet cord that Rahab used during her rescue is referred to as the cord of redemption. Jesus is our redemption! And He continues to rescue anyone who has the faith to believe He can - even when the walls are crashing all around.

The spies' presence in Jericho brought fear to the king, but it brought hope to Rahab. Today, the presence of Jesus brings fear to some and hope to many others. This story challenges me to be a "spy of hope." We have the opportunity to bring hope to those who are looking for a rescuer. That hope ... it starts at the manger.

How does this story challenge you?

December 6

Travel Plans

Boaz was the father of Obed
*(whose mother was **RUTH**).*
Matthew 1:5

Confession. I have a terrible habit of skimming portions of the Bible when it's very familiar or when I find it boring, like the genealogies. But when I read the Bible looking for specific ideas such as the character of God, leadership principles etc., I often see things I hadn't noticed before.

In reading the book of Ruth for today's Christmas character, I immediately started to skim through it. Ugh. I caught myself pretty quickly and started over. I slowed down, and this time I read it through the eyes of Christmas.

"So the two of them continued on their journey. When they came to Bethlehem..." (Ruth 1:19)

There it is! A trip to Bethlehem = Christmas!

In this story, "the two" are Naomi and Ruth, and Naomi was returning home. It was a lifetime ago when Naomi last lived there, and she was a different person then. She was married with two sons. She had a home and land before Bethlehem fell on hard times. Naomi's husband,

Elimelech, had moved his family to Moab, a place nothing like Bethlehem. Fear and a hungry belly drove him to a place of compromise. For Naomi, returning to Bethlehem wasn't going to be easy. She now had had no husband, no sons, no home, and no land to return to. Nevertheless, this grief-stricken widow decided to go home.

Ruth lived in Moab where they worshiped the gods, Chemosh and Baal. Part of the belief system included human sacrifices. Ya, nothing like Bethlehem. Naomi's son, Chilion, and Ruth got married. Ten years later, Ruth's father-in-law, brother-in-law, and husband were all dead, but Ruth remained loyal to Naomi. Even though Naomi tried to persuade Ruth otherwise, Ruth made a powerful declaration to Naomi.

"Don't ask me to leave you and turn back. Wherever you go, I will go; wherever you live, I will live. Your people will be my people, and your God will be my God." (Ruth 1:16-17)

This statement was not only a cultural commitment to Naomi, but Ruth was also surrendering her life to God. Little did she know that by honoring Naomi, she would one day carry a son who would be grandfather to King David *and* be included in the genealogy of Jesus!

You see, we make our plans, but the Lord directs our steps. (Prov 16:9)

Naomi planned to escape Moab, but the Lord directed her to redemption. God returned the land to Naomi, restored her reputation, and blessed her with a grandson!

Ruth planned to go glean fields for humble provisions. The Lord directed her to Boaz's field, where she was provided for and protected and blessed! She married Boaz, a good and honorable man. They had a son, Obed, David's grandpa. Ruth simply planned to do an honest day's work, but the Lord directed her to so much more!

What a life lesson! When we commit our lives to Jesus, we can know that He is always actively directing our steps.

If your Christmas plans don't go as expected, look for where the Lord may be directing you. He may be leading you to look inward for personal soul care, or He may be directing your steps to other opportunities. Wherever it is, it will be for your benefit and His glory - even if it means going back to Bethlehem!

December 7

Gift Exchange

*Salmon was the father of **BOAZ** (whose mother was Rahab).*
Boaz was the father of Obed (whose mother was Ruth).
Matthew 1:5

Christmas for the Herndons includes big family celebrations. One year, we hosted the Herndon Christmas dinner, so to help with everyone's Christmas budget, we played the Gift Exchange game. You've probably played a version of it yourself. This particular year we had a $20 limit to be spent at a hardware store. The ultimate prize is not the present we receive, but who gets the "nailed it" bragging rights for what they brought. This Christmas, it was Kate and the toilet seat!

In our story today, Boaz certainly nailed it! He's a wise, kind-hearted, honest, hard-working man of integrity. Boaz cares for and protects others, even foreigners who show up in his field. He's wealthy and generous. He's Judea's most eligible bachelor!

Boaz is known as a kinsman (family) redeemer. In Bible times, it was a close family member's responsibility to redeem (or purchase) the land for the one who lost it. The law therefore allowed Naomi, Ruth's mother-in-law and Boaz's relative, to redeem her land and legacy. Naomi's bad choices earlier in life had cost her dearly.

Nevertheless, Boaz stepped up! There was a shoe exchange for the purchase of Naomi's property. Shoes. Exchange. That captures a shopper's attention!

"Now in those days it was the custom in Israel for anyone transferring a right of purchase to remove his sandal and hand it to the other party. This publicly validated the transaction. So the other family redeemer drew off his sandal as he said to Boaz, "You buy the land."" (Ruth 4:7-8)

Boaz accepted the offer, and in the presence of witnesses, Boaz received the sandal as a sign of his acceptance and purchase of the property. The sale was legal and, the property now belonged to Naomi. Buying the land also meant marrying Ruth and fathering children in her name! The land would never be a part of Boaz's holdings, but Ruth's. That's quite a gift exchange! Boaz gladly paid for it. Yep, he nailed it!

This story describes all of us. People make stupid mistakes and bad choices. And sadly, we become the losers. We lose out on relationships, personal and moral integrity, monetary value, and more. We try to earn back what we have given away or even attempt to take it back. Sometimes we give up. We tell ourselves that we don't deserve it, that it doesn't matter. But the truth is, it does matter! And we *can* get it back! But not on our own. Like Naomi, we need a redeemer. We need someone to pay that price for us. Amazingly someone has! And it's paid in full!

Redemption is never cheap. Jesus was born so he could pay the price of sin for us. He literally "nailed it" to the cross. He exchanged His life for our sins. Jesus, our redeemer, is the best gift of all.

To experience Christmas to the fullest is to see the cross in the center of it. And like any gift, to benefit from it, we need to receive it.

December 8

It's Complicated

Jesse was the father of King David. David was the father of Solomon (whose mother was ***BATHSHEBA****, the widow of Uriah).*
Matthew 1:6

Jay and I took the newest member of his team out to lunch. I wanted to hear all about his fiancé. I wanted to learn about his interests and whether he prefers dark or milk chocolate. You know, the essential things. The three of us were having a great time, and the conversations were flowing until I asked if he had any siblings. He paused and simply said, "It's complicated."
Today as we look at Bathsheba and her story, I would describe it the same way; it's complicated.

Her story begins with a bath she was taking. Get it? Bath-she-ba. Anyway, King David saw her while she was bathing on her rooftop. He wanted her. He had her. Oops, she's pregnant, but she's another man's wife. Now what?

David came up with a plan. He brought her husband, Uriah, off the battlefield and sent him home to sleep with his wife. That would cover David's sin! Except Uriah wouldn't go home to the comfort of his wife while his soldiers were sleeping on the battlefield. Now what? David decided to eliminate the problem. He had Uriah killed in battle. (II Sam 11)

Really, David?

David marries Bathsheba. Their baby dies. She gets pregnant again. This baby lives, and he will one day be king. His name was Solomon.

My brain spins at reading this story, and I can only imagine Bathsheba having to live it. The king abused his power and betrayed his friend as well as the nation. He made Bathsheba an accomplice of his sin. Does that make Bathsheba guilty, too? I have a hard time reconciling that Solomon, one of the greatest kings ever, came from one of David's greatest failures. How does that happen? Were adultery and murder all part of God's plan? No!

It's complicated. Some things don't make sense and maybe never will. However, these things I do know:

- Our lives are intertwined, and we share stories: It's challenging to talk about Bathsheba without talking about David. Bathsheba's story would have been different if it hadn't been for David, and yet Bathsheba is a critical part of Jesus' story. My head is spinning again.
- Repentance and forgiveness bear fruit: David had to humble himself and admit his sin. Solomon was the fruit of David's repentance.
- God is in the restoration business: Bathsheba lost a baby and then gave birth to a king. Bathsheba is the one who continues the genealogy to Jesus, the ultimate King!
- And lastly, Jesus is a trustworthy King! -- David, not always.

Life is undoubtedly complicated. The good news of Christmas is that Jesus comes into messy, complicated situations! The question for us is this: Will we invite Jesus into our embarrassing mess? Do we truly believe He is trustworthy? Yes! 100 %! But sometimes, in the complicated mess, it's easy to forget.

December 9

Heaven and Earth

All of this occurred to fulfill the Lord's message through his prophet:
(ISAIAH)
Matthew 1:22

Growing up in a Pentecostal church, it wasn't uncommon for a church leader to shout a prophetic word to the congregation. The more specific the message, the more convinced I was that it came from the Lord. I remember feeling the awe and wonder of it all. I still do.

Isaiah is an Old Testament prophet, and his prophecies about the coming Messiah are VERY specific! Look at this. "The Lord himself will give you the sign. Look! The virgin will conceive a child! She will give birth to a son and will call him Immanuel (which means 'God is with us')." (Is 7:14)

Isaiah spoke this prophecy about 700 years before Jesus was born. He said it with such specificity and accuracy that it's as if Isaiah was speaking directly to the shepherds, Joseph, or Mary's family. For that matter, change the "she" to "you" in the latter part of that verse, and it's the angel's announcement to Mary. "You will give birth to a son and will call him Immanuel." Incredible! And that's not all.

Two chapters later, we read this prophecy: "For a child is born to us, a son is given to us. The government will rest on his shoulders. And he will be called: Wonderful Counselor, Mighty God, Everlasting Father, Prince of Peace." (Is 9:6)

I'm horrible at punctuation and grammar. (I thank the good Lord for editors!) But in this declaration from Isaiah, even I notice the present and future tense about the single subject.

He *is* born. He *is* given. He *will* be called.

Isaiah had such assurance of what was to happen. It was as if Jesus was born right then and there! He is born. He is given.

The Lord's Prayer says, "Your Kingdom come. Your will be done on earth as it is in heaven." (Matt 6:9-13 NKJV) Christmas was already "done" in heaven. Isaiah knew it, saw it, and declared it 700 years before it happened. Remarkable!

Advent is about waiting and expecting the Messiah. Seven hundred years is a very long wait. But Isaiah's prophesies did come to pass. And if the prophecies about Jesus's first arrival came to pass, then we can be assured that the prophecies about His second coming will as well!

It's been more than 2000 years in the second Advent period (the birth of Jesus to now). Every generation believes it will be the one to witness Jesus riding in on the clouds. I am no different. I earnestly believe that we will see it! We will be the ones to meet Jesus in the air! I can't wait to fly!

However, even if the second coming isn't for another 156 years, I am confident He is coming again!! It is planned in heaven. It will happen on earth.

December 10

Silence

***ZECHARIAH** and Elizabeth were righteous in God's eyes, careful to obey all of the Lord's commandments and regulations.*
Luke 1:6

As an assignment for Jay's doctoral program, he had to participate in a silent retreat. He started his silence at home early in the morning. Being unfamiliar with the concept of a silent retreat, I talked to Jay about many things. He finally broke his silence to explain "silence." Not only could he not speak, but the house had to be silent. Hmmm, that wasn't going to work for the kids and me. So, Jay retreated elsewhere.

Zechariah was on a silent retreat of his own. (Lk 1:5-22) On this day the priests gathered at the Temple in Jerusalem. Lots were cast (like a name drawing). Zechariah would burn the incense in the Holy place on the altar of incense. This duty was the most desired but also one of the most perilous. Before Zechariah burned the incense, other priests offered burnt sacrifices as payment for their sins and the sins of God's people. If the priests' hearts weren't right, they died.

God accepted the sacrifices. Zechariah lit the incense on the altar and prayed on behalf of his people. It was at this moment that an angel appeared. Gabriel stood before Zechariah! This is not the time or place that one would want to see an angel. Zechariah was terrified! But Gabriel quickly assured Zechariah not to fear.

The angel came to announce the soon-coming Messiah! Not only that, but God had heard Zechariah's prayer! He and Elizabeth would have a son! Woohoo! That's not all. Their son would prepare the nation for the arrival of the new king!

I don't doubt that Zechariah had been praying for both a Savior and a son. And God heard and answered his prayers in a way that Zechariah could never have imagined! I would therefore have expected Zechariah's response to be full of thanksgiving, but it wasn't. With a tone of disbelief, he replies, "How can I be sure this will happen? I'm an old man now, and my wife is also well along in years." (Lk 1:18)

The priests studied the messianic prophecies, so one would think Zechariah would have understood the magnificent message. But he didn't. You see, waiting can make one weary, whether it's for a son or for the Messiah.

Zechariah's disbelief caused his voice to be silent until the birth of his son. That's a long time not to speak, but hey, he was still alive! This silent retreat gave Zechariah much time to reflect, and I'm sure he carefully considered Gabriel's words. He probably reread the prophecies with a new perspective.

Nine months later, Elizabeth gave birth to Zechariah's son! The family couldn't believe what Elizabeth was going to name their baby boy. "So they used gestures to ask the baby's father what he wanted to name him. He motioned for a writing tablet, and to everyone's surprise, he wrote, "His name is John." Instantly Zechariah could speak again, and he began praising God! (Lk 1:62-64)

Did you notice Zechariah's first words? He didn't complain about being mute for nine months. Instead, he exclaimed the goodness of God! Hallelujah!

Perhaps this Christmas, the Lord is calling us to a silent retreat - to silence our voice of criticism, judgementalism, and disunity - to silence the chaos, fear, and hostility. Perhaps the Lord is calling us to gain a different perspective - His! Then we, too, can shout our own Hallelujah!

What needs to be silenced in your life?

December 11

Slay It

*When Zechariah's week of service in the Temple was over, he returned home. Soon afterward his wife, **ELIZABETH**, became pregnant and went into seclusion for five months.*
Luke 1:23-24

In the spring of 1985, my mother-in-law came to visit us in Las Vegas. She suspected I was pregnant and recommended I take a pregnancy test, so I did. No one was more shocked or surprised than me! I mean, we weren't planning on having kids yet. Joshua was born in December. With our second, Janae, it wasn't as easy. It was over a year before that little bun was in the oven, and I couldn't wait to tell my family, especially since she would be the first girl!

Elizabeth, the priest's wife, responded differently than me. She kept it a secret for five months. Elizabeth wasn't young; in fact, she was well beyond her childbearing years. And yet Elizabeth chose to keep this miracle pregnancy quiet. Commentators argue whether Elizabeth literally secluded herself from people or if she simply concealed her pregnancy. Either way, this was a significant time for Elizabeth and her Lord. Her time of seclusion provided an opportunity for reflection and contemplation. I'm sure she had to deal with past jealousies. It's difficult watching others live your dreams.

You see, jealousy is an ugly beast, but gratitude kills that beast.

In seclusion, Elizabeth proclaimed, "How kind the Lord is! He has taken away my disgrace of having no children." (Lk 1:25) Elizabeth's gratitude slayed the beast right on time! Little did she know that her proclamation would soon be tested.

Mary, the soon-to-be mother of Jesus, also secluded herself when she learned of her pregnancy. I love Elizabeth's response when her cousin Mary came to stay with her! "Elizabeth gave a glad cry and exclaimed to Mary, "God has blessed you above all women, and your child is blessed." (Lk 1:42) Elizabeth celebrates Mary and wasn't jealous that Mary's baby was "greater" than her own. Instead, she honors Mary's miracle with a joyful and grateful heart! Elizabeth passed the test!

Jealousy breeds jealousy. When Elizabeth killed that beast, it positioned her to raise her son confidently! John, who was later called John the Baptist, had a big task ahead of him, and Elizabeth raised him to embrace his own calling as a forerunner for Jesus. Jealousy would not have allowed that.

What a great lesson! When we are jealous of someone's gifts and calling, then we cannot fully function in our own.

As we are preparing for our own Christmas festivities, be aware of the beast of jealousy. Let's slay it when the perfect social media Christmas snapshot attacks us. Let's kill the beast when others have more presents under their tree or a grander spread at the table. Let's slay the giant when someone's lights are brighter and their Christmas bonus has more zeros. Let's slay it, I say! Slay it!

How do we do that? Like Elizabeth! We slay the beast of jealousy by being sincerely grateful for ALL that the Lord has done for us! Once we slay the ugly giant, we can truly celebrate what the Lord is doing in the lives of our friends, family, and neighbors, 365 days of the year!

December 12

Trust

*Gabriel appeared to **MARY** and said, "Greetings, favored woman! The Lord is with you!" Confused and disturbed, Mary tried to think what the angel could mean. "Don't be afraid, Mary," the angel told her, "for you have found favor with God! You will conceive and give birth to a son, and you will name him Jesus. He will be very great and will be called the Son of the Most High. The Lord God will give him the throne of his ancestor David. And he will reign over Israel forever; his Kingdom will never end!"*

Luke 1:28-33

Yesterday I mentioned my shock at learning I was pregnant with Josh. It was a lot for me to take it in, but Gabriel's message to Mary - WOWZA!

This engaged, teenaged woman was not only going to get pregnant, but her baby would be the Son of God! No parenting pressure there. But before she can parent, she has to survive the pregnancy, and I'm not just referring to the delivery. You see, a pregnancy outside of marriage was a capital offense in ancient times, punishable by stoning to death.

Another hurdle Mary faced was getting pregnant. Her one question to Gabriel was about how that would happen. (I would have had a lot more questions for sure!) Mary understood that this wasn't a conventional pregnancy, nor would it happen the traditional way.

The angel replied, "The Holy Spirit will come upon you, and the power of the Most High will overshadow you. So the baby to be born will be holy, and he will be called the Son of God." (Lk 1:34-35)

Mary's reply to the angel was uncomplicated and profound. "I am the Lord's servant. May everything you have said about me come true." And then the angel left her. (Lk 1:38) In short, Mary said YES! She didn't try to negotiate a deal or ask for time to consider her options. She. Simply. Said. Yes.

We can become so familiar with a story that it loses its impact. When I pause to consider this massive YES, I wonder how she did that? The answer is, Mary was prepared. She had been saying "yes" to God her whole life – yes to honoring Him and living a life of integrity and purity. It began as a child with the small everyday decisions. Would she obey her parents? Would Mary stay away from things that were dishonoring to the Lord? The bottom line is this, Mary made the right decisions - the right yes and the right no, one conversation after another. Every right decision built the foundation on which Mary's BIG YES could stand.

Mary was confident that if God asked, then He would be with her! The obstacles of shame, inherent pressures, or being misunderstood by family and society were of no consequence. This incredible young lady shows us what it means to "Trust the Lord with all your heart, do not depend on your own understanding. Seek His will in all you do, and He will show you which path to take." (Prov 3:5-6) Trusting God was woven into the fabric of Mary's relationship with God.

Mary trusted God enough to say yes, and it changed the world. Friends, if we desire to do big things for God, we too need to be prepared to say YES!

What is God asking you to trust Him in? Will you say yes?

December 13

Perspective

*Jacob was the father of **JOSEPH**, the husband of Mary.*
Mary gave birth to Jesus, who is called the Messiah.
Matthew 1:16

Today's Christmas character is one I don't remember ever hearing a Christmas message on, except in conjunction with his wife, Mary. Perhaps it's because we don't know a lot about him? Maybe because there are only so many weeks in Advent, and there are more prominent characters? I don't know. But I do know Joseph is a remarkable guy! Let's check out his story.

Joseph was engaged to Mary, but Mary gets pregnant by the Holy Spirit. What? Whoever heard of that? No one! It had never happened before. But Mary is pregnant, and Joseph is not the father! He didn't want to stone Mary, which was well within his rights, so instead, he quietly called off the engagement. Then Joseph has a dream. An angel explains to Joseph that Mary is telling the truth about her pregnancy and that he should marry her. (Matt 1:20)

So Joseph quickly marries Mary, and it's reasonable to assume that he then brings her to live in his home. Joseph honored the Lord and his wife, and Mary remained a virgin throughout her pregnancy. OK, I'll say it, this is not your typical honeymoon! Joseph is to be commended.

After Jesus was born, the Lord spoke to Joseph again in a dream. An angel told Joseph to leave Bethlehem because King Herod was looking to kill baby Jesus. Joseph listened and quickly obeyed. Off to Egypt they went. (Matt 2:13)

After a couple of years there, the Lord again spoke to Joseph in a dream and said that it was safe to return to the land of Israel. As Joseph had done before, he quickly obeyed and led his family home. Joseph would have one more dream, and this one would lead them specifically to Nazareth.
(Matt 2:20-23)

God knew what He was doing when He put those two together. In a time when women were little more than mere property, Joseph treated Mary like royalty and respected God's call on her life. Joseph is the man!

Even so, I'm sure Joseph struggled just like the rest of us. We can read Joseph's story with the whole Christmas perspective in just a few minutes. It's a beautiful story! But remember, this was several years of Joseph's life, not just a few chapters.

Have you noticed that God works on a need-to-know basis? We don't always like that, but Joseph shows us how to deal with it. Joseph lived each day under the direction of God's last command to him. He trusted that God's plan made more sense than his own perspective, and that's all Joseph needed to know! That's really all any of us need to know.

So what about our own story? We all have one. And our stories are part of a bigger story. We may never completely understand it because we don't have God's perspective. But this we can be sure of, He's working it all together masterfully!

How does this change your perspective of your own story?

December 14

I Wonder

*In the sixth month of Elizabeth's pregnancy, God sent the angel Gabriel to Nazareth, a **VILLAGE** in Galilee. Luke 1:26*

Confession. I have a sickness. I call it Opinionitis (O•pin•yon•i•tis). It's when I exhaust too much energy worrying about the opinions of others, and at times it has been paralyzing. With help I've been able to overcome the condition, although I will admit that it still pops up from time to time.

I wonder if Mary or Joseph had this sickness? You see, opinionitis could consume their thoughts. What would the villagers think about Mary's pregnancy and her so-called explanation or Joseph's decision to marry Mary anyway? Opinionitis would assume Joseph was the one to get Mary pregnant. Opinionitis would worry about the shame Mary and Joseph brought upon their families and community. I wonder if Mary or Joseph were frightened about any of this? Or is it just me?

I wonder if Mary and Joseph were concerned about the family reaction? That would undoubtedly be a difficult conversation - trying to explain Mary's unexpected pregnancy and Joseph's need to move up the wedding date. Mary and Joseph had said "Yes!" to God, but we don't know how nauseous they felt or how many tears they cried.

The "YES" is easier when you have a healthy support system. But sometimes villagers (friends and family included) can be less than enthusiastic about us following Jesus. It can seem dangerous or unpractical or maybe even a little crazy to them.

Mary and Joseph were confident in their decision to obey the Lord. They did not allow the villagers' opinions to dictate their decisions, and neither should we. Faith conquers fear, but not always right away. My friend Jodi calls this "doing it scared".

One can be both confident and "doing it scared" at the same time. We also can be confident in what the Lord is asking of us, and at the same time, do it scared. When I step into the pulpit, I'm both confident and doing it scared. When I lead an event, I'm confident, and I do it scared.

The weight of the responsibility and opinionitis is what scares me. Doing it scared is admitting that I CANNOT do it without the Lord! Doing it scared is what keeps me reliant on the Holy Spirit.

So friends, as a new year is just weeks away, let's enter it like I imagine Mary and Joseph entered their new life - doing it scared but with confidence in their God.

- We can be confident that the Lord is still on the throne and in control! There is nothing that happens in this world that He is not aware of or surprised by.
- We can be confident that the Lord in us is greater than the evil around us.
- We can be confident that God's love for people is deeper, wider, and higher than we can ever imagine.
- We can be confident that as we make our plans, the Lord is directing our steps.

- I can be confident … *you fill in the blank.*

I wonder what this next year will look like if we don't let opinionitis or any other fears stand in our way.

I wonder what the Lord can do with an army of strong and courageous believers, even if we are still a little scared.

December 15

Unlikely People

*At that time the Roman emperor, **CAESAR AUGUSTUS**, decreed that a census should be taken throughout the Roman Empire. All returned to their own ancestral towns to register for this census. And because Joseph was a descendant of King David, he had to go to Bethlehem in Judea, David's ancient home. He traveled there from the village of Nazareth in Galilee. He took with him Mary, to whom he was engaged, who was now expecting a child.*
Luke 2:1, 3-5

Taking a journey late in pregnancy isn't fun. I had carried Josh to term, and we were awaiting his arrival. It was late December and my sister, Cheri, flew to Las Vegas to wait with us, and she was anxious to meet our little guy. One gets bored sitting ... waiting ... wondering ... is today THE day? Jay doesn't "sit" well, so he decided we should go to Mt Charleston to play in the snow. They played. I waddled like a penguin. But at the end of the day, I had the comfort of a nice warm car to ride home in. On the other hand, Mary had a donkey? A mule? A cart? Walked? We don't know. I do know that NONE of those options are comfortable, especially when you're pregnant!

I can imagine the frustration that was directed at ol' Caesar Augustus. The Jewish people were already feeling the oppression of the Roman government. They were being pushed beyond their limits, and now

Joseph had to travel several days to get to Bethlehem with his very pregnant wife. It would take several days to get there. Ugh!

Joseph was probably thinking, "this certainly can't be part of God's plan!" - or at least I would have thought that. And yet Bethlehem *was* God's plan, and God used an unlikely character to get Mary and Joseph there. Was Caesar Augustus aware that God was using him to usher the King of Kings into this world? Uh, that's a big NO and a good lesson for us.

Friends, sometimes God uses unlikely people to get us to where we need to be. Like Mary and Joseph, the circumstances and timing may seem horrible. The "whats" and "whys" may be plentiful. And perhaps the situation is even beyond our control - just like going to Bethlehem wasn't optional for Mary and Joseph.

This story challenges us to acknowledge the unlikely characters in our stories. They often push and prod and make our lives uncomfortable. They can hurt our feelings and make us mad. We often don't share the same belief system or have the same political views. It can be confusing and frustrating, and to be honest, I haven't always been very receptive when these people are allowed into my life. I am a work in progress. Nevertheless, God uses these unlikely individuals to get me where He wants me to be - relationally, emotionally, physically, and even spiritually.

As this part of our journey has us looking inward, let's remember that God's ways are not our ways, but He is *always* working for our good.

How does this change your perspective of the unlikely people in your story?

December 16

Opportunities

So it was, that while Mary and Joseph were there, the days were completed for her to be delivered. And she brought forth her firstborn Son, and wrapped Him in swaddling cloths, and laid Him in a manger, because there was no room for them in the inn.
Luke 2:6-7 NKJV

At the beginning of each year, Jay and I participate in a road trip where we visit 100's of pastors in Northern California and Nevada. On one particular trip we had arrived at our designated hotel. It was late, and we were looking forward to sleep, only to be told, "Sorry. You don't have a reservation and there are no rooms available." Fortunately we had smartphones, and we located accommodations elsewhere. Mary and Joseph had no such conveniences.

Tradition tells us that Mary and Joseph walked from inn to inn. All the innkeepers told them, "There's no room in the inn!" and the door is slammed for dramatic effect. Then one innkeeper or his wife took pity and allowed them to lodge with the livestock. At least they'd have a roof over their heads - just ignore the smell. It's plausible that it happened this way, but we can't know for sure.

These innkeepers do get a bad rap for closing the door in Mary's face and rightfully so! If they only knew who was standing at their door. If just one had invited Mary and Joseph in, our Christmas pageants would portray the role of the innkeepers very differently!

I wonder if any innkeepers were kicking themselves for not making room for just two more after their neighbor's stable became famous. I wonder if the stable owner miraculously had an available room so Mary and the newborn King could recover in a more comfortable space? I wonder if they were oblivious the entire time?

Jesus invokes the innkeeper image in Rev 3:20. "Look! I stand at the door and knock. If you hear my voice and open the door, I will come in, and we will share a meal together as friends." Our Christmas character and this verse are the inspiration for the iconic paintings of Jesus knocking at a door in the dark of night. What a powerful reminder that we each have our own innkeeper opportunity! Jesus is knocking. Will we invite him in?

My conclusion: What missed opportunities! Or were they? Certainly for some! But could it also be that hosting the birth of Jesus wasn't their opportunity to miss? Jesus left the glories of Heaven to be born in a cave (stable) and laid in a feeding trough (a manger). That was the plan.

I kick myself over my own missed opportunities, but this causes me to reevaluate, "Was it mine to miss?" Sometimes, yes. I missed out because my fears, immaturity, or impatience got in the way. But other opportunities were not mine to miss! They were meant for someone else.

That's quite liberating! The Lord's warehouse of opportunities is limitless. I'm excited that some are for me, and I'm thrilled some are for you! When it's not all about us, we are free to rejoice when someone else gets the job, ministry opportunity, house, or whatever else we think should be ours.

Let's pray that we will always keep open the door of our lives to Jesus! He's knocking. Pray we say 'yes' to opportunities the Lord gives us. Pray we won't wallow over missed opportunities, especially those that are not ours to begin with.

December 17

There's Hope

Now there were in the same country ***SHEPHERDS*** *living out in the fields ... And suddenly there was with the* ***ANGEL*** *a multitude of heavenly host praising God and saying: "Glory to God in the highest, and on earth peace, goodwill toward men!"*
Lk 2:8,13-14 NKJV

On Christmas morning, I'm like a kid who is excited about what's under the tree, but the excitement isn't for the gifts I will be receiving (although Jay is a great gift-giver). I'm excited to share all the goodies with their intended recipients, and I can't wait to share in their joy!

This verse is that same idea but on steroids. The angels had been privy to seeing God doing some really BIG things - parting the Red Sea, tumbling the walls of Jericho, sending down fire from heaven, and maybe even being eyewitnesses to some of the creation.

But this ... this was bigger than all of that! This news was fireworks finale big! And the angels got to deliver it! I can imagine their eagerness as they were waiting. "Is it time, Lord? Now is it? Can we go yet?"

Then finally, like music to their ears, God said GO! And in an instant, 10,000 angels appeared in the sky. Ten thousand voices were praising God and saying, "Glory to God in highest heaven, and peace on earth to those with whom God is pleased." (Lk 2:14) How glorious that must have been!

I can picture the shepherds in the field watching out for predators that would like a lamb chop for dinner. Perhaps they were warming themselves by the fire when SUDDENLY an angel appeared, and God's glory was radiating all around them. The angel tells the shepherds about a baby that was born. This baby is going to save the world! Then the shepherds are given instructions on where to find the baby. And SUDDENLY there are now 10,000 angels! These lowly shepherds had an eyewitness account to heaven's exuberant praise!

The shepherds hurried off to see this newborn king whose name is Emmanuel - God is with us. I can imagine them running and trying to process this incredible announcement! *"What? Are you kidding me? I didn't think this would happen in our lifetime! God is with us? How?"*

Christmas is the story of the incarnation: God became flesh. The incarnation is one of the most challenging Christian doctrines to explain, but here it is. Jesus was completely God and completely man. He wasn't a little of both but 100% of each. And God chose the shepherds to be the first visitors to see God on the earth! Here He was, accessible to ordinary people! This was extraordinary! And it still is!

After the shepherds encountered the angels, met Mary and Joseph, and worshipped baby Jesus, they had to go back to their sheep. The shepherds' situation hadn't changed on the outside, but on the inside they had a new hope for what was coming. Hope births patience and peace, and peace changes our perspective.

We all need hope! Not a wishful thinking kind of hope, but a solid guaranteed kind of hope. That's the hope Jesus offers! That's why we celebrate Christmas, and Advent helps us remember the whys. And that's a Merry Christmas!

Where in your life do you need Jesus and hope?

December 18

Searching

When the ***WISE MEN*** *saw the star, they were filled with joy! They entered the house and saw the child with his mother, Mary, and they bowed down and worshipped him. Then they opened their treasure chests and gave him gifts of gold, frankincense, and myrrh.*
Matthew 2:10-11

One Christmas, I showed my granddaughter, Norah (7), my olive wood Nativity set from Bethlehem. She asked me, "Gramma, why do you have the wise men there? They weren't even there yet!" I was proud of my little love. Norah was entirely right. The wise men (AKA Magi or Kings) were not at the stable with the shepherds. They arrived at Mary and Joseph's home in Bethlehem two to three years after Jesus was born.

That was a long trip.

The Magi were astrologers and scholars, hence their title as wise men. They studied the stars and apparently the scriptures as well because they connected the star to the Old Testament prophecies. These prophecies talked about a future king who would rule the world.

That's smart.

The star appeared twice. The first sighting was in the East. This directed the wise men to Jerusalem where they met with King Herod who in turn sent them on to Bethlehem. The star then appeared again, confirming the location. The Magi had therefore set out and completed the journey without the consistent presence of the star.

That's confidence.

The wise men traveled for a significant length of time which would have required adequate preparation. They probably left their families behind, and there were no guarantees that they would survive a journey of that length.

That's commitment.

The Magi brought gifts: Gold, frankincense, and myrrh.

- Gold, a gift for a king.
- Frankincense, a gift for a priest.
- Myrrh, used at a burial.

That's revelation.

Jesus, the King of kings (Rev 17:14), was crucified for our sin. He was buried with a perfumed ointment made from myrrh and aloes (Jn

19:39) and now sits at the right hand of God as our High Priest! (Heb 4:14) Today, Jesus is interceding on our behalf!

That's extraordinary!

Why did God choose to reveal the Savior's birth to the wise men? Because they were searching.

Today, humanity is looking. The question is, for what? Peace - health - safety - blame - truth - happiness. Whatever it is, Jesus wants to have a conversation. The Lord spoke to Mary through an angel, Joseph in a dream, and wise men through a star. This story reminds me that God speaks to us differently as well. He talks to each of us in ways that we will hear Him.

The Lord still speaks to some in dreams, others in nature, and some through people. He speaks in circumstances and even in the silence. The Lord communicates with us through the 66 books of the Bible. We may not understand it all, and that's okay. But like the Magi, God is wanting us to seek Him!

During this Advent season, what are you searching for?

December 19

Not everyone

*Then **HEROD** called for a private meeting with the wise men, and he learned from them the time when the star first appeared … the wise men returned to their country by another route, for God had warned them in a dream not to return to Herod.*

Matthew□ 2:7,12 □

Not everyone was excited about this newborn king, Herod being one of them. Well, to even say Herod was not excited is an understatement. Herod did not like competition or to feel threatened in any way. So to hear there was a new king in town, well, that wasn't going to sit well!

The Roman Emperor appointed Herod to be king over the eastern Mediterranean including Judea. He is often called Herod the Great but not because he was a great leader. History reports that he was a tyrant: vicious, mean, untrustworthy, and just evil. No, he wasn't a great leader, but he was a great builder. Jay and I have made several trips to the Holy Land where we have seen and touched some of the structures Herod built! They are pretty remarkable.

I remember visiting Herodion in 2009. It is the remains of one of Herod's palaces, and the ingenuity of that structure is incredible. It's built on a man-made mountain top to take advantage of the view of Jerusalem and the Judean desert. The palace is seven stories, complete with banquet rooms, courtyards, a luxurious bathhouse, and expansive balconies with grand vistas. Yep, he was a great builder.

What I couldn't help to notice was how close this summer palace was to Bethlehem. It's located 7 miles south of Jerusalem and only 3 miles southeast of Bethlehem which is easily visible from the palace. Right below the extended balcony is a field. Perhaps a shepherd's field? I don't know. But it got me thinking.

Luke tells us that the glory of the Lord was shining around the first angel when he appeared to the shepherds. Then the multitude of angels appeared. I'm pretty sure they also had the glory of the Lord upon them. It doesn't take much light to light up the night sky. I think God's glory would have been visible for many miles, especially from Herod's palace with its 360-degree views!

Even if Herod had been at one of his other fourteen palaces when the angels appeared, this particular palace would not have been left unattended. Someone was there! Yet no one else seemed to have seen it. By God's design, I'm sure.

I remember standing there thinking, "Jesus was born right under Herod's nose, and he didn't even see it." And then I smiled. It still makes me smile.

Not everyone today is excited about the birth of Jesus. The hostility against the church is rising. In some places, the political and social climate is devastating, just as it was during King Herod's reign. Even so, FEAR NOT! Jesus said, "I will build my church and the powers of hell will not conquer it." (Mt 16:18) Christ's promise remains true: His Church and His people will not be destroyed! They weren't then, and they won't be now!

Jesus was born to die so that we may live.

How does this truth affect your outlook on our world today?

December 20

The Good King

The wise men asked, "Where is the newborn king of the Jews? We saw his star as it rose, and we have come to worship him." King Herod was deeply disturbed when he heard this, as was ***EVERYONE*** *in Jerusalem.*

Matthew 2:2-3

Everyone is today's Christmas character on our ADVENTurous journey.

This verse has puzzled me a bit. Why would everyone in Jerusalem be disturbed at the news of a new king? Herod was a horrible king who took the throne! He made everyone's life miserable! Why wouldn't they want Herod out?

I'm sure most did. But at what cost? Herod was old by now, and I'm sure he was getting meaner by the day. He was incredibly insecure and easily threatened. Herod had two of his sons killed for treason because the people of Judea liked his boys better than they liked him. Herod was extremely jealous. So when news of a new king came along ... ya, everyone in Jerusalem was disturbed.

The people feared the price that Herod would make them pay for the arrival of another king. Herod was only looking out for one person, himself. Jealously and selfishness do not make for a good king! The good news of Christmas is that Jesus *is* a different kind of King!

Jesus is not evil. He is loving and just.
Jesus is not inconsistent. He is faithful and true.
Jesus is not unethical. He is righteous and holy.
Jesus is not ruthless. He is merciful and forgiving.

There are still many people today who are disturbed by the idea of Jesus. There could be several reasons for this response. Perhaps past experiences have skewed their perception of who Jesus is. I get it. It can be a challenge to reconcile a loving Jesus with the evil that exists. Maybe some fear the price they would have to pay, like being sent somewhere they don't want to go, giving up their freedom, and not having fun anymore. Maybe the idea of having to lose relationships or being harassed isn't worth it. Whatever the reason, their conclusion is - following Jesus costs too much.

Jesus wants to change those misperceptions. However, they aren't the only ones. It's also *me*, or should I say, *we*?

After following Jesus my whole life, I discover that I can still have misperceptions of my own. I've struggled with feeling like I'm not good enough. I've wondered how Jesus can love me when I don't even like me. I count my blessings and then feel unworthy of them. Even though Jesus loves me just the way I am, He doesn't want me to continue with these misguided feelings. He loves me enough to expose my wrong belief system and to teach me the truth. Jesus wants to reveal the truth of who He is to all of us!

I am more than confident that Jesus is a good King! I will follow no other ... no matter the cost.

What is Jesus revealing to you?

December 21

The Promise

That day the Spirit led ***SIMEON*** *to the Temple. So when Mary and Joseph came to present the baby Jesus to the Lord as the law required, Simeon was there. He took the child in his arms and praised God, saying, "Sovereign Lord, now let your servant die in peace, as you have promised. I have seen your salvation, which you have prepared for all people.*

Luke 2:27-31

My Grandma Clark lived a long life. She died just weeks after turning 101, but she was ready to "go home" long before then. Grandma loved Jesus, and she was ready to be in heaven with Him. She also had a daughter and husband waiting for her there. When someone else passed away, she'd comment, "It should have been me. It should have been me." I should have replied, "Maybe next time, Grandma." That would have made her laugh.

I think of my grandma when I read about Simeon. Both lived a long life. They were both ready to leave this one and start the next in the presence of the Lord.

Although my grandma was ready years before her passing, Simeon was holding out for God's promise that he would see God's salvation before he died. That's quite a promise!

Simeon was a man who walked with the Lord and was led by God's Spirit. On this particular day, God's Spirit led Simeon to the Temple. At the same time, Mary and Joseph were bringing baby Jesus to the Temple to dedicate Him to the Lord.

The Temple was a busy place with people coming and going as they brought offerings and sacrifices as well as to pray and worship. I imagine it was sort of like a crowded Christmas production: people in costumes, choir members taking their places, kids waving to their parents, and guests jockeying for the best seats in the house. I call it organized chaos. But somehow Simeon noticed Mary and Joseph in the sea of people. Or was he drawn to the babe in arms? However it happened, Simeon was standing with the newlyweds and their precious baby. He took Jesus in his arms and knew, without question, that he was holding the Promise.

Incredible! Simeon saw salvation in a baby. Did he know it would be a baby? Did Simeon ever assume he would meet God's Promise in person in such an intimate way? Or did Simeon expect to see his deliverer from afar, and that was enough for him?

I don't know. But I do know that God is faithful to keep His promises! And He often answers them in ways that are beyond what we could ever dream or imagine!

As Simeon held Jesus in his arms, he began to prophesy and asked the Lord to allow him to die in peace. Simeon had peace knowing his sins would be forgiven and peace in knowing there was hope for future generations. Simeon didn't need to see how it was going to happen. Seeing the One who would accomplish all these things was enough.

Friends, when we know the *Who,* we can have peace in the *how.*

My prayer for this next year is that we will see as clearly as Simeon and that we, too, would be led by the Spirit in everything we do. I don't want us to miss anything the Lord desires show us.

What is your prayer?

December 22

Waiting Expectantly

ANNA *came along just as Simeon was talking with Mary and Joseph, and she began praising God. She talked about the child to everyone who had been waiting expectantly for God to rescue Jerusalem.*

Luke 2:38

Confession: Sometimes, I'm surprised when God answers my prayers.

Years ago, my cousin needed her gallbladder removed. The family gathered around her, and I prayed that the Lord would heal Cortney and that she would not require surgery. I knew without a doubt that God could heal my cousin! Cortney went to the hospital and had a final scan. To the doctor's amazement, there were no stones, and they canceled the surgery! The doctors weren't the only ones amazed. I was like, "Really?"

I was sure about the "He could" but lacked confidence in the "He would." That is a bit embarrassing to admit, but this experience strengthened my faith. Jesus proved He could, and He did. 100%!

I wonder if Anna was surprised to see the answer to her prayers in Simeon's arms?

Anna was married for seven short years when her husband died, and she remained a widow the rest of her days. She spent her time at the Temple, fasting and praying whenever it was permissible to do so. No doubt, she prayed for her country, her people, *and* for a deliverer to come.

When Anna saw Simeon talking with Mary and Joseph, did she know right away that her deliverer had just arrived? Or did it take a few moments to process? I imagine Anna's understanding was much like Elizabeth's when Mary went to stay with her. She just knew. That's the Holy Spirit speaking!

The Bible says that Anna had been waiting expectantly. She knew God would answer. It was just a matter of time. Just as Anna waited expectantly for the first Advent, we wait expectantly for the second. Jesus will come again. It's just a matter of time.

In the meantime, waiting expectantly is a brilliant way to live! It's the perfect combination! Waiting without an expectation of an ending is exhausting. Expecting without clear direction is nerve-wracking. Either one on its own can breed unrest, but together, they offer peace.

We can be at peace in our waiting if we have an expectation that the wait will come to an end. Likewise, I can be at peace with my expectations when I'm patient enough to wait.

I like it! I need it! I'm adding "Waiting Expectantly" to my New Year's goals list. Care to join me?

In what area of your life would "waiting expectantly" give you peace?

December 23

Amazing Love

*For God so loved the world that he sent his only son, **JESUS**.*
John 3:16-17

I LOVE my kids and my grandbabies! I can't imagine any circumstance in which I would sacrifice any of them for anyone, but God did precisely that. God knew the only way to save this broken world was to send His One and only Son to us.

Jesus left the comforts of heaven for a stable and manger; He had no place to lay His head and traded His heavenly form for a human body. But Jesus willingly did so because He loves us. Love motivated Jesus to grow and learn from childhood to manhood, live among us, and die an excruciating death for us.

Growing up in Sunday School, we were taught that Jesus loved us so much that He died for our sins. I'm one to accept what I'm being told, even if it doesn't make a lot of sense to me. Yet in the back of my mind, I wondered why? Why did Jesus have to die? It does sound extreme but consider this: Someone has to pay.

Let's say you get a new car for Christmas, and then you get into an accident. Someone is paying the price for that accident. Either an insurance company pays, or an individual pays out of pocket. If the accident is ignored, then you are paying by driving a wrecked car or paying Uber to drive you around.

The payment for sin is death. Every one of us has sinned. Even the nicest and purest among us has sinned, and the only way to absolve that sin is death. That might seem severe, but we don't get to make the rules. And as much as we'd like to, sin just cannot be ignored either. Someone must pay.

God *SO LOVED* us that He sent Jesus to pay the price for our sin. That was the plan from the moment Adam and Eve sinned in the garden.

Jesus is the Promise of the prophets. He is the Hope of the women in His genealogy. Jesus is the Rescuer for people past, present, and those to come.

The price Jesus paid was once and for all! Jesus died, so we don't have to! However, there is a condition to this gift - we must receive it. How? We receive God's gift by admitting that we are sinners in need of a Savior. This can be another difficult concept to grasp. Yet here it is. We are all born with sinful, selfish natures. Think about it. We teach children to share, to tell the truth, and to be honest. It's our nature to do the opposite. We are all guilty of sin and we need a Savior. There is no shame in this confession! As a matter of fact, the Bible tells us that heaven rejoices! (Lk 15:7)

So, my fellow sojourners, as we near Christmas day, my gifts are wrapped, menus are planned, and family is arriving soon. Perhaps yours are as well. As we are settling into our Christmas celebrations, let's be ever so mindful that Christmas was an amazing sacrifice ... done in amazing love.

December 24

To: Us

*For a child is born to **US**, a son is given to us.*
Isaiah 9:6

It's Christmas Eve! Families everywhere have their traditions on when they open their Christmas presents. For the Herndons, it's Christmas morning - but not before the family climbs on our bed to open stockings and we have our Christmas breakfast which Jay and the kids prepare!

One Christmas morning, I found Janae kneeling at the Christmas tree, taking scrupulous notes. When I asked her what she was doing, she informed me she was taking inventory by tallying the number of presents each of us had under the tree. Inventory became an annual tradition for her, and I can't blame her. Everyone wants to see their name on a package!

As we are looking for our name on a Christmas package, I hope we can see by now that we have been given the greatest gift of all time, Jesus! Our names were written in red when God gave His son, To: Us!

I'm in awe when I ponder that God willingly sacrificed His son so you and I can be in a relationship with Him, right now and into eternity!

So travelers, now that we have reached our destination on this ADVENTurous Christmas journey, let's unpack a few things.

The first Advent was met with heaven and earth rejoicing. There was also rejection and fear. The Second Advent will be the same. Jesus encourages us this way, "Don't let your hearts be troubled. Trust in God, and trust also in me. There is more than enough room in my Father's home. If this were not so, would I have told you that I am going to prepare a place for you? When everything is ready, I will come and get you, so that you will always be with me where I am." (Jn 14:1-3)

Christmas is marked on our calendars, and that makes our celebration of the 1st Advent easy. However, Jesus says this about His second coming: "No one knows the day or hour when these things will happen, not even the angels in heaven or the son himself. Only the Father knows. And since you don't know when that time will come, be on guard. Stay alert!" (Mk 13:32-33)

If this makes you feel a bit unsettled, I get it. It's intense! But just like good parents who give their kids a "heads-up", our Heavenly Father is giving us a major heads-up! Jesus is coming again!

"For the Lord himself will come down from heaven with a commanding shout, with the voice of the archangel, and with the trumpet call of God. First, the believers who have died will rise from their graves. Then, together with them, we who are still alive and remain on the earth will be caught up in the clouds to meet the Lord in the air. Then we will be with the Lord forever." (1 Thess 4:16-17)

I love castles and mansions, and I cannot wait to see the pearly gates as well as emeralds, sapphires, and other precious stones that adorn its foundation and walls - and, of course, the streets of gold.

Heaven will be a place where every tear will be wiped from our eyes. There will be no more death or sorrow or crying or pain! (Rev 21:4)

And most of all, heaven will be a place where we will be with the One who loves us the most.

"Yes, I am coming soon!" -Jesus
(Rev 22:7)

Any Day

Prayer of Dedication

I have prayed that the Lord speak to you through this journey. If you don't have a personal relationship with Jesus, or perhaps you have neglected your relationship with Him, that could change today! All you need to do is talk to Jesus. Tell him what you are thinking and feeling.

If you're not sure what to say, pray something like this.

> *Dear Jesus,*
> *Something is stirring in me, and I believe you want to have a relationship with me. I want to have a relationship with You, too. I admit that I am a sinner, and I need a savior. Jesus, please be my savior. Thank you for leaving Heaven to be born in a manger. Thank you for loving me so much that you would pay the penalty of my sin by dying on the cross. Thank you for giving me a new life. Teach me how to be like you, Jesus. I'm yours.*
> *Amen.*

Welcome to the family of God!
Teri

Made in the USA
Las Vegas, NV
02 November 2021

33544416R10046